3-D THRILLERS!

SHARKS

DUTTON CHILDREN'S BOOKS
NEW YORK

Masters of

Shark. The very name can strike terror in many people's hearts. But sharks deserve much more than our fear. They also deserve our admiration and respect. These mysterious predators of the deep have been swimming in the world's oceans for over 450 million years—that's 200 million years before the dinosaurs! For the last 200 million years, some sharks have remained nearly unchanged, rising to the top of the food chain. Today there are more than 375 different shark species, and more are still being discovered.

BONELESS FISH

Unlike most fish, whose skeletons are made of bone, sharks' skeletons are made of a tough, bendable material called cartilage—the same elastic material inside our ears and noses. Cartilage is flexible and lightweight, so sharks can swim, twist, and turn quickly when chasing prey.

HE DEEP

Our word "shark" comes from the German word *Schurke*, which means "greedy parasite" or "scoundrel." Sailors first used the word to describe people who had swindled them.

COUSIN RAY

Although there may seem to be little family resemblance, the shark's closest relatives are rays, skates, and chimeras. Like their shark cousins, they also have skeletons of cartilage. Together they make up the class Chondrichthyes (con-DRIK-thees).

Most fish have an air sac called a swim bladder that helps keep them afloat, or buoyant, but sharks do not. Instead, their livers are full of oil, which is lighter than water; this helps them float. Even with their livers, sharks are still heavier than water and must keep swimming to stay buoyant.

THAT'S ROUGH

Not only are sharks' mouths full of teeth, their skin is, too! A shark's body is covered in tiny, toothlike scales called denticles. If you rub a shark's skin one way, it feels smooth, but if you rub it the opposite way, it is rough like sandpaper.

BETTER TO

Sharks are the deadliest, most successful predators in the ocean. When they hunt, all of their senses go to work, and they are just about unstoppable. First a shark hears a sick or wounded creature struggling from more than a mile away. Swimming toward the sound, the shark picks up the prey's scent in the water and tracks it to its source. A shark also uses a special sense of touch. Sensors called lateral lines run the length of its body and can sense movement and vibrations in the water. So a shark can "feel" something without even touching it.

EYE GUARD

By getting close to and hanging on to thrashing, struggling prey, a shark can get poked in the eye. To protect themselves, some shark species have a special eyelid called a nictitating membrane that covers the eye just before attack. Other sharks, like the great white, roll their eyes back into their heads.

SWIFT SWIMMERS

Even the shape of a shark's body helps make it a champion predator. Almost all sharks have a curved and tapered torpedo-shaped body, which allows it to glide smoothly—and swiftly—though the water after its prey.

SIXTH SENSE

Sharks may not have ESP, but they do have a sixth sense. Tiny pores in a shark's snout called ampullae of Lorenzini can pick up the electrical pulses that all living things give off. This helps the shark pinpoint the exact location of its prey so it can strike with amazing accuracy.

FIND YOU WITH!

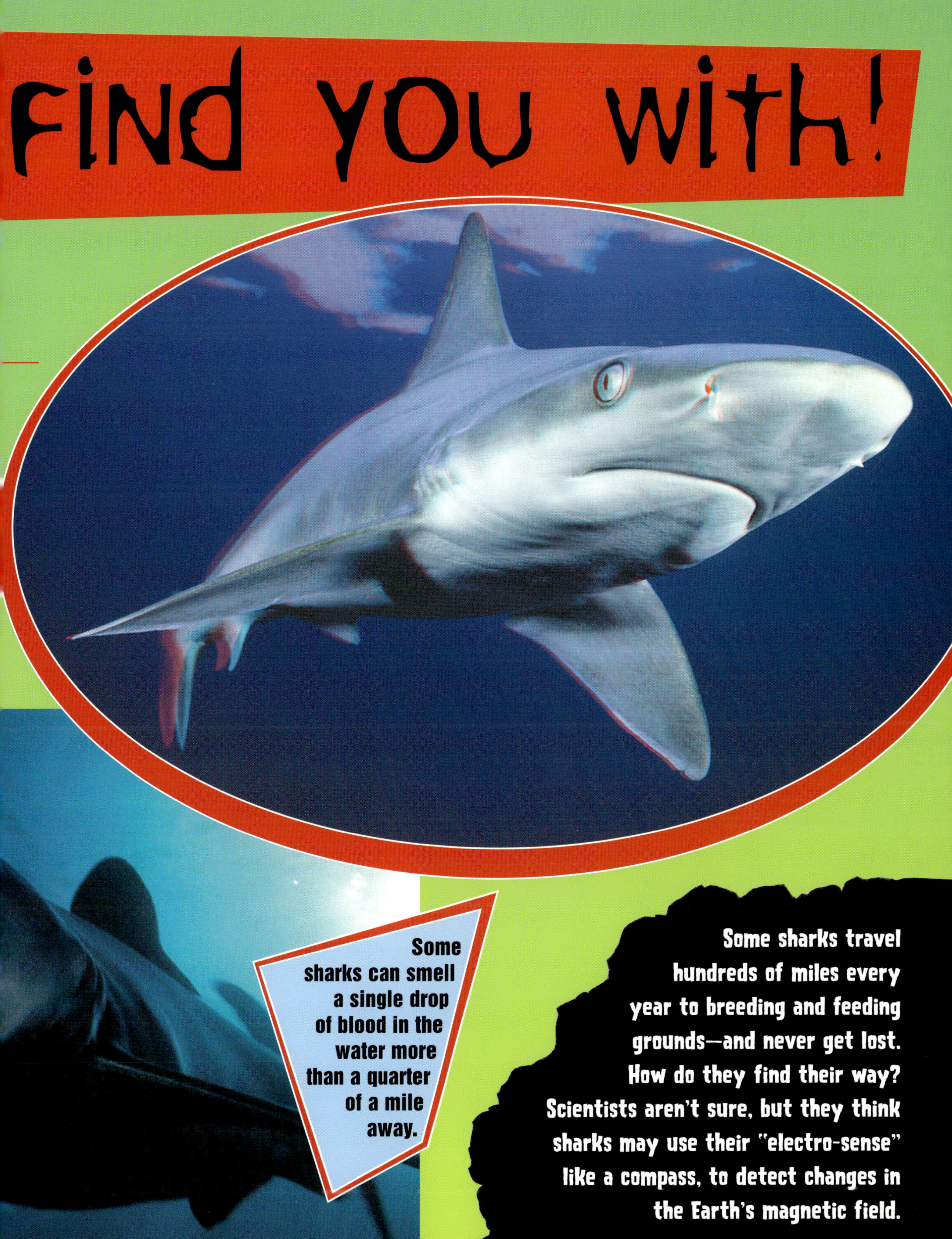

Some sharks can smell a single drop of blood in the water more than a quarter of a mile away.

Some sharks travel hundreds of miles every year to breeding and feeding grounds—and never get lost. How do they find their way? Scientists aren't sure, but they think sharks may use their "electro-sense" like a compass, to detect changes in the Earth's magnetic field.

Better to Eat

The dinner menu is quite similar for most kinds of sharks. They prefer smaller fish (including other sharks) and invertebrates such as squid. Bottom-dwelling sharks, like the wobbegong, however, eat shrimps, crabs, and other crustaceans that live near the ocean floor. Large sharks, like the great white and the bull shark, also feed on marine mammals. Sharks often prey on sick or wounded animals, since they are easier to catch. Unlike most sharks, tiger sharks are notoriously nonpicky about what they eat—they will swallow just about anything they can get their jaws on.

DENTAL CARE

Every time a shark eats, some of its teeth either break or fall out. Luckily, every time a tooth falls out, a replacement tooth from the row behind is waiting to take its place. Some sharks have ten or more rows of teeth and can go through over 20,000 teeth in a lifetime!

TAKE A BITE

One of the weirdest feeders of all is the cookie-cutter shark. Its round mouth is specially designed to take cookie-sized bites out of larger animals like whales and dolphins. The cookie-cutter shark is about as long as a skateboard, and its "cookie bites" are not fatal.

YOU with!

FILTER FEEDERS

The largest sharks in the ocean—the whale shark, megamouth, and basking shark—eat some of the ocean's smallest food: microscopic plants and animals called plankton. Their mouths act like giant strainers to filter tiny plankton out of the water. The 30-foot-long basking shark (right) filters 330,000 gallons of water an hour—enough to fill a large swimming pool.

Some of the more unusual "foods" found in the tiger shark's stomach include license plates, shoes, weights, tin cans, and an alarm clock.

SUPPER IN A SNAP

A shark's jaws are not connected to its skull, so it can move both its top and bottom jaws out and forward, allowing it to open its mouth REALLY wide. The shark then snaps its powerful jaws shut, just like a trap.

The good, the b

The more than 375 different shark species come in a variety of sizes and shapes. The biggest, the whale shark, can grow more than 50 feet long, while the smallest, the pygmy shark, is less than 6 inches long and can fit in the palm of your hand. Sharks can be spotted or striped, flat-bodied or round—some deepwater sharks even glow in the dark!

FUNNY FACE

Hammerhead sharks, with their strange, **T**-shaped heads, are easy to recognize. Their eyes, which are on either side of their broad, flat heads, give them excellent all-around vision. These sharks use their heads to pin prey, such as stingrays, to the ocean floor.

The fastest shark is the shortfin mako, which can swim up to 30 mph in short bursts.

SPOT THE SHARK

Many bottom-dwelling sharks, like this tasseled wobbegong, are covered in spots, blotches, or stripes so that they blend in with plants and rocks on the seafloor. This helps them hide from enemies and also catch unsuspecting prey.

d, and the ugly

HORNSHARK

The hornshark gets its name from the two sharp spines that stick out from its dorsal fins. The spines make predators think twice before attacking. This 3-foot-long shark lives on the ocean bottom off the coast of California and Mexico.

MAKE YOUR MIND UP, SPOTS OR STRIPES!

Baby zebra sharks have black and yellow stripes, but as the sharks grow, the markings change into pale brown spots. The adults are therefore sometimes called leopard sharks.

Many sharks are dark on top and pale underneath. When seen from above, they blend in with the dark waters below, and from underneath they match the sunlit waters above.

The heavyweight

Introducing, in this corner, the most infamous shark to swim the ocean, the most feared predator in the sea—the great white. In the far corner, the largest shark in the world, also known as the "gentle giant"—the whale shark. How do these two heavyweights of the shark world measure up?

JAWS—TRUTH EXPOSED!

In 1975, the movie *Jaws* made many people afraid to go into the water. But the great white shark in that movie could never have existed in real life. The filmmakers built a mechanical shark with extra teeth and wrong-size fins; it would sink if it were real. When real sharks were filmed, small, model divers made them look bigger than they were.

GREAT WHITE

Scientific name:
Carcharodon carcharias

Size: Also known as the "white death" or the "white pointer," the great white is the largest flesh-eating shark. It is about 18 feet long and weighs over 2 tons.

Coloring: It has a very distinctive two-tone coloring. Its upper body is blue to gray, while its underbody is much lighter, even white.

Range: The great white lives in cool waters in subtropical and temperate seas.

Diet: With its 2-inch-long serrated teeth, the great white eats fish and sea mammals like seals and sea lions.

Scientists now believe that many of the attacks blamed on the great white are actually committed by the bull shark.

WHALE SHARK

Scientific name: *Rhincodon typus*

Size: It is named after its size. Measuring over 45 feet long and weighing more than 13 tons, the whale shark is the largest shark, and the largest fish, in the world.

Coloring: On top it is blue gray, but underneath it is white. Its skin is camouflaged with distinctive white spots and bars to help it blend in with the surrounding water.

Range: The whale shark lives in warm waters on either side of the equator, both in the open ocean and near the shore.

Diet: Plankton. The shark flushes huge mouthfuls of water over its gill rakers (walls of spongy mesh inside its throat). The gill rakers act as a sieve, trapping the plankton for the shark to swallow.

BIG MOUTH, TINY TEETH

The whale shark's mouth is lined with thousands of tiny teeth, each one about the size of a grain of rice. The teeth aren't used for eating. Actually, biologists aren't sure what, if anything, the teeth are used for.

HUMAN-INFESTED

Despite the frightening attacks you may have seen on the movie screen, shark attacks on humans are extremely rare. There are about fifty attacks reported each year, out of which only two or three are fatal. In fact, humans have more to fear from mosquitoes than from sharks. Bites from malaria-carrying mosquitoes kill 2 to 3 million people every year, making mosquitoes a million times more lethal than sharks. There are four "usual suspects" in most shark attacks on humans. They are the tiger, bull, great white, and oceanic whitetip shark.

More people are injured by coconuts falling on their heads than are injured by sharks!

MY MISTAKE

Many shark attacks on humans are a case of mistaken identity. To a shark, a diver wearing a wet suit and flippers, or a surfer on a surfboard, can look like its favorite food—a seal or a sea turtle.

WATERS

POLLUTION

Sharks are also threatened by pollution. Chemicals in the water kill the fish they eat, while oil spills destroy important breeding grounds. Sharks mature very slowly and give birth to few young. Often sharks are killed, either by overfishing or pollution, more quickly than they can reproduce.

HUMAN ATTACK!

The truth is, we are far more dangerous to sharks than they are to us. Every year, 200 million sharks are killed by humans—that's 275,000 sharks a day! They are fished for their meat, skin, teeth, oil, and just for fun. Many sharks are accidentally caught in nets meant for other fish.

TACKY SOUVENIRS

Sharks are killed for their jaws as well, which are removed and sold as souvenirs. If you are tempted to buy one, remember where it came from.

Chances are a shark will never attack you, but here are some ways to avoid close encounters of the shark kind.

Don't swim where sharks have been seen.

Don't swim alone. Sharks will attack a lone swimmer before threatening a group.

If you see a shark, swim calmly to the boat or shore. Splashing and panicking will only attract a shark.

Remember, the ocean is their home—you are just a visitor.

S.O.S.—Save O

So many sharks are killed each year that several kinds, including the great white, blue, and basking shark, are in big trouble. They are classified as threatened species, meaning their numbers are dwindling so rapidly that conservationists warn they could soon be in danger of dying out altogether. If shark species died out, all of ocean life would suffer. As top-of-the-food-chain predators, sharks keep many fish populations in check; as scavengers, sharks help keep the oceans clean.

HEALTH SHARKS

Sharks don't lose many days to sickness because they don't often get diseases. Finding out why sharks are so healthy could one day help us discover how to avoid serious diseases like cancer.

SPIRITS OF THE DEEP

Sharks are important symbols for native peoples around the world. In Hawaii, people believed that the shark god Kamohoali would help lost fishermen by leading their canoes through fog and mist. Some Pacific Islanders believe sharks are the spirits of their dead ancestors.

ur Sharks

Aquariums also play a part in helping sharks. By allowing visitors to get a close-up view of live sharks, they help us understand that sharks are worth far more alive than dead.

WHAT IS BEING DONE?

Many marine biologists and conservation groups are working very hard to make sure we don't hunt our sharks to extinction. Biologists study sharks in their natural environment to learn more about their behavior and life history. The more we know about sharks, the more we can do to help save them. Conservation groups spread the word about sharks in danger, pressure governments to pass laws protecting sharks, and set up underwater nature reserves where sharks can live without danger of being fished by humans.

We must help change the shark's reputation as a ruthless man-eater so it will be respected and preserved.

Discovery Kids™, which includes Saturday and Sunday morning programming on Discovery Channel®, Discoverykids.com, and the digital showcase network, is dedicated to encouraging and empowering kids to explore the world around them.

Published in the United States 2000 by Dutton Children's Books,
a division of Penguin Putnam Books for Young Readers
345 Hudson Street, New York, New York 10014
www.penguinputnam.com

Editor: Sarah Ketchersid Authors: Lynn Gibbons and Chris Coode
Designers: Leah Kalotay and Susi Martin

Picture Credits:
Front cover; page 1; page 3 bottom right; page 4 bottom right; page 5; page 6 bottom left; page 9 middle right; page 10 top left; page 12; page 13 top right, bottom left; page 16: Oxford Scientific Films.

Back cover; page 2; page 3 top left; page 4 top left; page 6 top right; page 7; page 8; page 10 bottom left: BBC.

Page 9 top, bottom; page 10 top left; page 11 bottom right; page 13 top left; page 14 bottom left; page 15: Planet Earth.

Page 14 top right: Jamie Oliver

3-D images produced by Pinsharp

Printed in China
First Edition
ISBN: 0-525-46405-0